What Is Self-Control?

Self-control is when ...

1   I stop doing wrong or harmful things to myself or others.

2   I keep myself from doing something wrong, even when it's difficult.

3   I control angry feelings, so that I don't hurt others.

4   I react to things in a calm way or sometimes just ignore it.

Why Should I?

Match the text to the pictures to find out why it's important to have self-control. Then fill in the speech bubbles with what each person might be saying.

Self-control is learning to control our emotions, which can help us to control our thoughts and behaviors.

Self-control is an important skill for everyone to learn.

It means having control over your own actions.

It's learning right from wrong and practicing choosing what is right.

My Controlling Jar

Check out this fun idea! And once your jar is full, treat yourself to a favorite snack.

1 Take a jar that you don't use anymore.

2 Decorate it with stickers, ribbons, glitter or colorful papers.

3 Collect some big rocks.

4 Every time you control your words, your emotions, your temper or your actions, take a rock and write on it with a marker what you controlled.

5 Then place it in the jar.

6 Check on your jar every so often to watch your progress.

7 Stop to think about how it feels to be more in control of yourself.

How am I doing?

Things to Control

There are different ways of controlling yourself. See some of the examples below and color the pictures where the children are using self-control.

CONTROL YOUR **THOUGHTS:**

CONTROL YOUR **ACTIONS:**

CONTROL YOUR **EMOTIONS:**

CONTROL YOUR **HABITS:**

4

From an Early Age

If you can learn self-control from an early age, then you will feel better about the choices that you make when you get older. Notice how the choices change in importance as you grow older?

Match the pictures with the text examples:

ADULT

BABY

TEEN

KID

CHOOSING CLOTHES

CHOOSING A WIFE

CHOOSING A SNACK

CHOOSING TO SAY "NO!"

Rate Yourself

Here's a fun little chart to help you rate your level of self-control.

This can help you get started with practicing more control.

Color in the appropriate box at the bottom of the page to see how you fared.

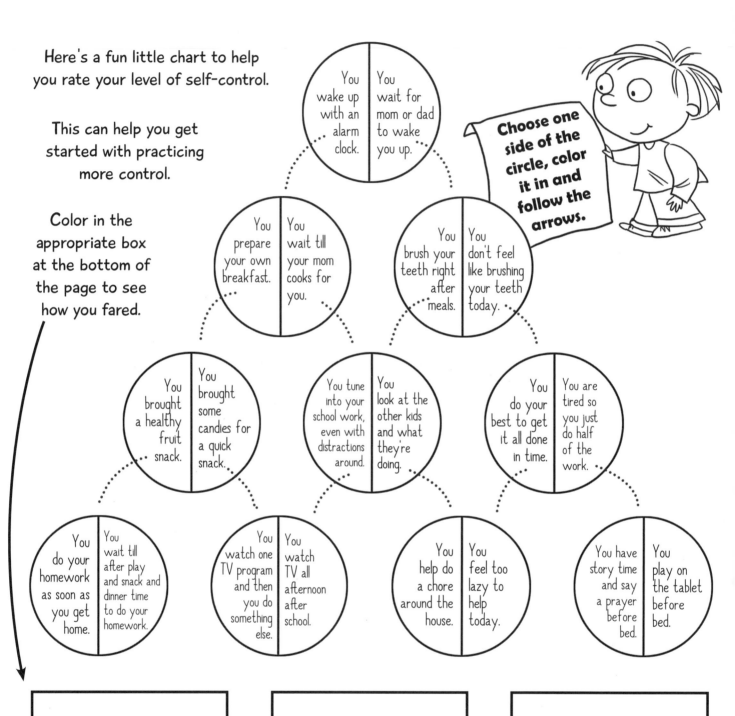

Choose one side of the circle, color it in and follow the arrows.

You wake up with an alarm clock. | You wait for mom or dad to wake you up.

You prepare your own breakfast. | You wait till your mom cooks for you.

You brush your teeth right after meals. | You don't feel like brushing your teeth today.

You brought a healthy fruit snack. | You brought some candies for a quick snack.

You tune into your school work, even with distractions around. | You look at the other kids and what they're doing.

You do your best to get it all done in time. | You are tired so you just do half of the work.

You do your homework as soon as you get home. | You wait till after play and snack and dinner time to do your homework.

You watch one TV program and then you do something else. | You watch TV all afternoon after school.

You help do a chore around the house. | You feel too lazy to help today.

You have story time and say a prayer before bed. | You play on the tablet before bed.

If you got more than 7 of the left sides colored, you are well on your way to being self-controlled. Congratulations!

If you got at least 5 of the left sides colored, you are already practicing self-control and making good progress.

If you got less than 3 of the left sides colored, you have a great opportunity to start learning to be self-controlled.

Understand Why

How do you feel when someone tells you "no" or "later"?
It can be difficult because you want it your way. Here are some reasons
why you may get a "no" or "later" response. Understanding why might help
make things easier for yourself.

Unscramble the words in the boxes, then use them to fill in the blanks.

1
YGOUN

2
PIENESVEX

3
SLIGOUREI

4
MITE

5
THEYHAL

6
HINTGS

7
NEDNALP

1. YOU'RE STILL A LITTLE TOO _ _ _ _ _ _.
2. IT MAY BE TOO _ _ _ _ _ _ _ _ _.
3. BECAUSE OF YOUR FAMILY'S _ _ _ _ _ _ _ _ _ BELIEFS OR CULTURE.
4. YOU DON'T HAVE _ _ _ _ RIGHT NOW.
5. IT'S NOT _ _ _ _ _ _ _ FOR YOU.
6. YOU HAVE PLENTY OF OTHER _ _ _ _ _ _ _ INSTEAD.
7. THERE IS SOMETHING ELSE _ _ _ _ _ _ _ _ FOR YOU TO DO.

Choose Your Options

Match up the cupcakes and toppings.

If you have been told that you can't have something, one way to control your mood is to find another possible solution.

Here are a few ideas that you could try out.

STAY CHEERFUL EVEN IF YOU ARE NOT ALLOWED, AND SAY ...

... FOR YOUR TURN.

ASK IF YOU CAN DO SOME EXTRA CHORES ...

... TO MAKE THE OTHER PERSON SMILE.

IF THE ANSWER WAS A "MAYBE"...

... "I WOULD LIKE IT, BUT THAT'S OK."

BE PATIENT AND WAIT ...

... TO EARN MONEY TO BUY ONE.

FIND SOMETHING ...

... ELSE TO DO INSTEAD.

OFFER TO DO SOMETHING NICE ...

... SWEETLY ASK AGAIN LATER.

Tempting Scenarios

Draw 3 of the examples from the list, that have happened to you.

Some things can be tempting to do just because you feel like doing it, or it's the easy way out. But be careful because it's not always what's best for you.

1 YOU WANT TO PLAY WITH YOUR FRIEND, BUT YOU HAVE HOMEWORK TO FINISH FIRST.

2 YOU NOTICE OTHERS WHO HAVE TOYS OR GADGETS THAT YOU WOULD LIKE.

3 YOU HAVE TO TAKE OUT THE TRASH, BUT YOU'D RATHER PLAY INSTEAD.

4 YOU GO TO A RESTAURANT AND SEE LOTS OF DELICIOUS FOOD YOU WANT TO EAT.

5 YOU WANT TO GO TO BED, BUT YOU HAVEN'T BRUSHED YOUR TEETH YET.

6 YOUR FRIEND GETS TO DO SPECIAL ACTIVITIES OR GO PLACES THAT YOU WISH YOU COULD GO TO.

A Bible Verse

Above all things, guard your heart.
Proverbs 4:23

**Read the clues to fill in the blanks.
Then write each word on the lines provided to put
the Bible verse in order.**

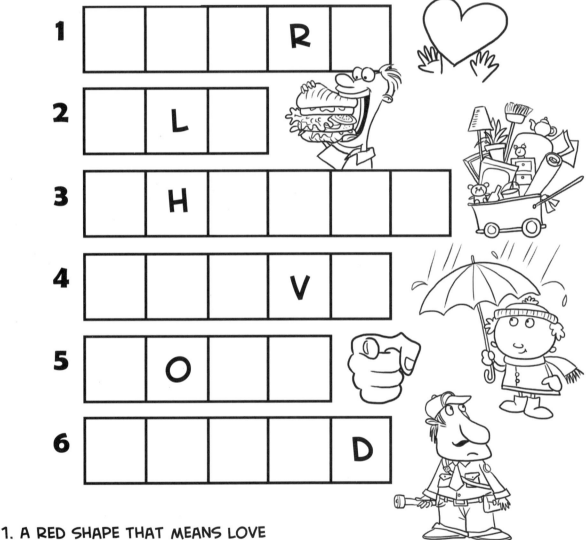

1. [ ][ ][ ][R][ ]

2. [ ][L][ ]

3. [ ][H][ ][ ][ ]

4. [ ][ ][ ][V][ ]

5. [ ][O][ ][ ]

6. [ ][ ][ ][ ][D]

1. A RED SHAPE THAT MEANS LOVE
2. A SHORT WORD THAT RHYMES WITH BALL
3. ANOTHER WORD FOR STUFF OR BELONGINGS
4. OPPOSITE OF UNDER
5. OPPOSITE OF "MY"
6. SOMEONE WHO PROTECTS AND DEFENDS

_ _ _ _ _ _ _ _
_ _ _ _ _ _, _ _ _ _ _
_ _ _ _ _ _ _ _ _!

Good or Bad
Hard or Easy

Read the scenarios and circle the two letters that you think best describes them.

G = good / B = bad
H = hard / E = easy

G B H E

Do what the other kids are doing so that they don't make fun of you.

G B H E

Save up your money to buy what you really need, even though you see a favorite toy on sale.

G B H E

You have to study for a test, but you decide to sleep a bit longer instead.

G B H E

Try something new that you've never done before.

G B H E

The sign says "One cupcake each!" but you're hungry so you eat one more.

G B H E

Say you're sorry even though it's embarrassing.

Notice how the hard things almost always match up with the good.
This shows that it's often difficult to control ourselves and to do what is right.

Learn Self-Control

Find the word in each balloon that does not belong.
Write it on the lines to fill in the blanks.

CIRCLE
CONTROL
SQUARE
1

STOP
BOOK
PENCIL
2

HAND
LEG
COULD
6

WRONG
DESK
BED
5

FOOTBALL
BASEBALL
MYSELF
3

HARMFUL
SHIRT
BELT
7

SPAGHETTI
DOING
ICE CREAM
4

UGLY
PRETTY
OTHERS
8

SELF-_____ IS WHEN I _____ _____ FROM
         1   2   3

_____ SOMETHING THAT IS _____ OR THAT
   4   5

_____ BE _____ FOR ME OR _____.
   6   7   8

12

Throughout Your Day

Draw some examples of what you know how to control throughout your day.

IT'S IMPORTANT TO PRACTICE SELF-CONTROL, EVEN IN THE SMALLEST OF THINGS. SO THAT WHEN IT COMES TIME ...

... TO WORK ON THE BIG THINGS, YOU WILL ALREADY HAVE A HEAD START AND IT WILL BE EASIER FOR YOU.

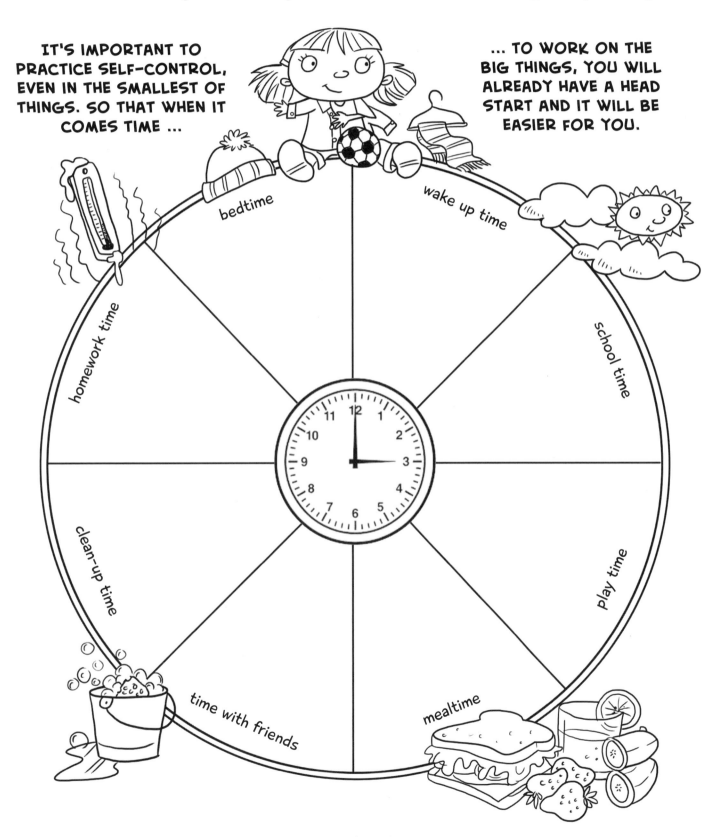

bedtime

wake up time

homework time

school time

clean-up time

play time

time with friends

mealtime

Ollie's Lessons

THE TOOTHPASTE TUBE

Tubes of toothpaste are very efficient little things. You can squeeze out only as much as you need in one go. You can turn it upside down and the toothpaste stays in. It keeps the toothpaste from drying out, and it's also a safe way to keep germs from getting in. But a long time ago, toothpaste came in jars or containers and everyone in the family dipped their brushes in. Toothpaste tubes are great, but there is still one small problem ...

... once the toothpaste is out, there is no way to put it back in. That sounds a lot like when we don't control ourselves. We might say or do things that we are sorry for later, but there is no way to undo them. For example, we can't take back mean and unfriendly words, even if we say that we're sorry. Those words will be remembered and can take a long time to heal in someone's heart. That's why it's important to control ourselves before we make the wrong choices.

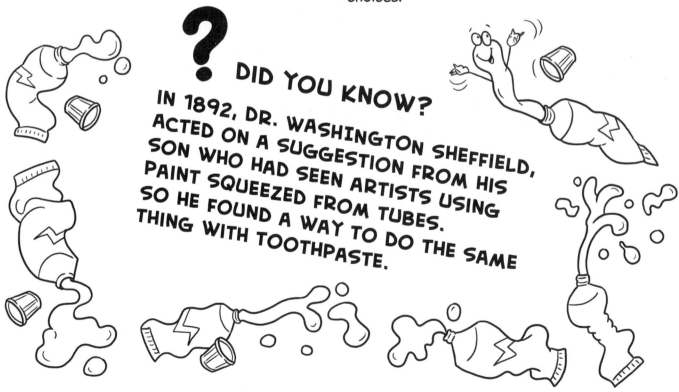

? DID YOU KNOW?

IN 1892, DR. WASHINGTON SHEFFIELD, ACTED ON A SUGGESTION FROM HIS SON WHO HAD SEEN ARTISTS USING PAINT SQUEEZED FROM TUBES. SO HE FOUND A WAY TO DO THE SAME THING WITH TOOTHPASTE.

Color your own toothpaste patterns.

Try it out!

1 Take a paper plate and a tube of toothpaste. Then squirt the toothpaste onto the paper plate. Experiment with different pressures or speeds and see how it comes out.

2 Next, try to put it all back in the tube. How is that working out for you?

3 Then, think about what you can do before you lose control and say or do the wrong things, or squeeze out all the toothpaste. Remind yourself that you'll have to clean the mess afterwards and it will not be easy.

You will need:
- a tube of toothpaste
- a paper plate

What positive words would you like to come out of your mouth? Write down some of the first things that come to mind.

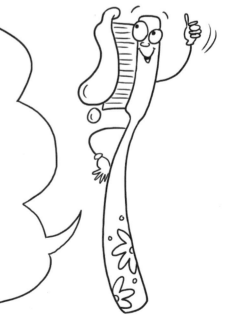

Illustrate a Bible Story

Read the Bible story on self-control
and have fun illustrating it in the boxes.
(Genesis 2:4-3:24)

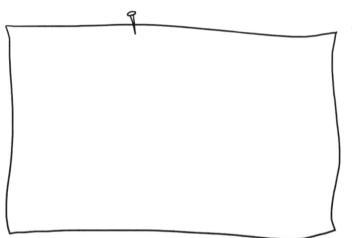

THE FIRST BEAUTIFUL PEOPLE GOD MADE WERE ADAM AND EVE. GOD GAVE THEM EVERYTHING THAT HE HAD CREATED, SO THEY COULD ENJOY IT; PUPPIES AND KITTENS, LIONS AND BEARS, EVEN APPLES AND POMEGRANATES.

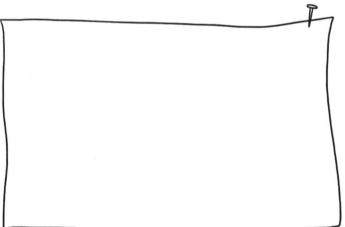

SPEAKING OF FOOD, THEY COULD PICK AND EAT FROM EVERY TREE IN THE GARDEN, EXCEPT FOR ONE SPECIFIC TREE THAT GOD TOLD THEM NOT TO EAT FROM.

AFTER SOME TIME, ADAM AND EVE GOT CURIOUS ABOUT THE FRUIT THEY COULDN'T EAT. ONE DAY, A SNAKE TRICKED EVE INTO TAKING A BITE.

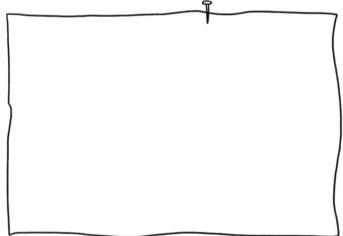

THEN SHE GAVE ADAM A TASTE TOO. WHAT HAD THEY DONE? NOW THEY FELT REALLY BAD AND KNEW THAT GOD WOULD NOT BE HAPPY WITH THEM FOR DISOBEYING HIM.

Story Application

I'M ALLIE! I'M READY TO HELP YOU APPLY GOD'S WORD TO YOUR OWN LIFE STORY.

Adam and Eve knew that they were not supposed to eat the **FRUIT** from the tree that God told them about. But when a slithery **TEMPTING** snake said that it was okay, they **LISTENED** to him instead. They didn't practice **ENOUGH** self-control to walk **AWAY** from doing wrong and **INSTEAD** chose to eat the fruit that looked so **GOOD**. They made a sad mistake by disobeying and so had to leave God's beautiful garden. They broke the perfect world that God had made. It hurts us in different **WAYS** when we can't **CONTROL** ourselves.

Find the bolded words from the text above, in this word search.

```
T M H Y W J O T P W E P G V F
Z E A M Y V X C B W W L V J R
G H M G O O D I R D P G Y W F
A D W P R B N C O N T R O L R
S R A U T S K G F L V W P K I
X W Y X Q I D G Z I D O W O U
H C S P S Y N S C S J Z R B T
I G A K X T E M P T I N G F B
A D U J M Y L A W E Y N C F J
X A W L P G M R I N S T E A D
B J Z M N Q M A F E N L W Z P
E N O U G H P U G D E V B T U
U C I G B S Q A L U R D S V N
D K T V I W O D I H K Q Y D O
A W A Y R X M Q I Q U N K J T
```

17

Coloring Page

Color in the Bible story.

(Genesis 3:6)

GOD TOLD ADAM AND EVE THAT THEY COULD EAT ANY FRUIT IN THE GARDEN EXCEPT ONE, BUT THEY DIDN'T CONTROL THEMSELVES AND ATE IT ANYWAY. THIS MADE GOD SAD.

Find Your Way

Emily needs to buy some bread at the bakery, but she feels like going to the candy store instead. Can you help her control herself and do the right thing?

React or Respond

If we can't control something, and we let our emotions take over, we will often **REACT** in a negative way.

But if we go slow and think about things first, we will be able to **RESPOND** instead, and handle the situation wisely.

FINDING A SOLUTION THAT WORKS

GETTING UPSET

BEING RELAXED

STAYING CALM

BEING OVERLY SENSITIVE

BEING GRUMPY

SHOWING PATIENCE

PUSH FOR MY OWN WAY

Draw a line from the descriptions that best fits the characters.

Play and Do

Try out these simple exercises or games to help you practice self-control.

1 Put a non-melting favorite dessert on a bowl in front of you. Practice self-control by waiting five minutes before you eat it, while sitting and watching it.

2 Ask your dad or mom for a bag of chips. Practice self-control by eating 3 chips every day. See how many days the bag of chips lasts.

3 When you're in the middle of watching your favorite TV show, see if you can practice self-control by turning it off five minutes before the end.

4 The next time your brother or sister says something mean, practice self-control by not saying anything in return. Instead, walk out of the room and do something to distract yourself.

Road to Progress

It helps to have some sort of plan to follow when you want to start a new habit or make progress in a certain area. Since we're on the topic of self-control, list some ways that you could do better with that?

SOMETHING I WILL TRY NOT TO DO:

1

Fill in the boxes with the different steps that you want to take towards having more self-control.

2

SOMETHING I WILL DO INSTEAD:

3

SOMETHING I WILL TELL MYSELF:

You can chart your progress by coloring in the boxes once you've passed that stage, or placing a sticker on top.

I WILL PRACTICE THIS EVERY DAY:

4

You'll feel better that you were able to practice using more self-control in your life.

Did you know?

Others will notice a change in you!

THE FINAL RESULT THAT I WANT:

5

Flip and Flop

He who controls others may be powerful,
but he who can control himself is even stronger.

Prayer Time

Asking for God's help can help you to control your emotions and give you the extra strength to make wise choices.

Fill in the blanks to make these your own prayers.

Dear God, I am having trouble controlling my tongue. Sometimes I say _____ things. Please give me more of Your _____ so that I can think and pray before I speak and be _____ in the things I say to others. Amen.

Dear God, please help me not to be tempted to _____ and make wrong choices because of my lack of self-control. Give me the strength to choose the good and to _____ _____. Amen.

Dear God, sometimes I have a difficult time controlling my actions. I _____ _____ . Please help me to have more of Your Holy Spirit so that I can please You with my actions and instead choose to _____ _____. Amen.

Dear God, when I want _____ _____ or to do other things like _____ that my friends get to do, please give me patience and help me to realize that _____ and that You're in control, so that I can trust You with it. Amen.

Answer Sheet

From an Early Age - Page 5

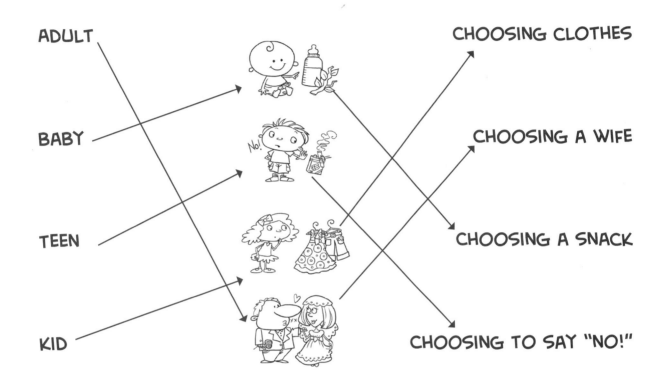

ADULT

BABY

TEEN

KID

CHOOSING CLOTHES

CHOOSING A WIFE

CHOOSING A SNACK

CHOOSING TO SAY "NO!"

Understand Why - Page 7

1. You're still a little too **young**.
2. It may be too **expensive**.
3. Because of your family's **religious** beliefs and culture.
4. You don't have the **time** right now.
5. It's not **healthy** for you.
6. You have plenty of other **things** instead.
7. There is something else **planned** for you to do.

Choose Your Options - Page 8

A Bible Verse - Page 10

1	H	E	A	R	T
2	A	L	L		
3	T	H	I	N	G	S
4	A	B	O	V	E
5	Y	O	U	R	
6	G	U	A	R	D

Complete sentence: *Above all things, guard your heart.*

Learn Self-Control - Page 12

(1) <u>Self-control</u> is when I (2) <u>stop</u> (3) <u>myself</u> from (4) <u>doing</u> something that is (5) <u>wrong</u> or that (6) <u>could</u> be (7) <u>harmful</u> for me or (8) <u>others</u>.

Story Application - Page 17

```
T M H Y W J O T P W E P G V F
Z E A M Y V X C B W W L V J R
G H M G O O D I R D P G Y W F
A D W P R B N C O N T R O L R
S R A U T S K G F L V W P K I
X W Y X Q I D G Z I D O W O U
H C S P S Y N S C S J Z R B T
I G A K X T E M P T I N G F B
A D U J M Y L A W E Y N C F J
X A W L P G M R I N S T E A D
B J Z M N Q M A F E N L W Z P
E N O U G H P U G D E V B T U
U C I G B S Q A L U R D S V N
D K T V I W O D I H K Q Y D O
A W A Y R X M Q I Q U N K J T
```

Find Your Way - Page 19

React or Respond - Page 20

Prayer Time - Page 24